The Unexpected Aviary

The Unexpected Aviary

Poems by L. R. Berger

DEERBROOK EDITIONS 2003

PUBLISHED BY
Deerbrook Editions
P.O. Box 542
Cumberland, Maine 04021-0542

FIRST EDITION

ISBN: 0-9712488-2-6

Manufactured by Sheridan Books, Inc.

Book design by Jeffrey Haste
Cover painting by Roger Haile
Photo of the author by Amy Sloane

Acknowledgments

My gratitude for the fellowships, residencies and support I have received from the National Endowment for the Arts, the New Hampshire State Council on the Arts, PEN New England, the MacDowell Colony, Hedgebrook, the American Academy in Rome and, most abidingly, the Blue Mountain Center.

I am also grateful to those editors of anthologies and journals who first published and believed in this work, and to Cicely Buckley at Oyster River Press who published a selection of these poems in *Sightings* as part of the chapbook series of New Hampshire poets, *Walking to Windward*.

My deepest appreciation and gratitude to all those who have so generously encouraged and loved this book into being over many years, especially Pamela Alexander, Harriet Barlow, Mary Blaine Campbell, Teresa Cader, Martha Collins, Jane Cooper, Sanda Ileuscu, Patricia Gianotti, Karen Latuchie, Cassandra Medley, Jennifer Moye, Alice Nye, Stephen Tapscott and Patricia Wilczynski.

Lastly, I extend my thankfulness to Roger Haile for his cover image, and to my publisher, Jeffrey Haste, who believes the art of book-making to be sacred work.

for Jane Cooper

Fling the emptiness out of your arms
into the spaces we breathe: perhaps
the birds will feel the expanded air
with more passionate flying.

—Rainer Maria Rilke

Table of Contents

Acknowledgments

IV

I

The Birds That Are Not in Our Hands

Call it desire,

to make a life
out of all I had,

a handful of feathers
surrounding a body of air

I whispered into, *birrrd*—

flying off at will
past the arc of eyes

and returning
with new colors.

I wanted words
to be the body,

still, what I had
were feathers and hands

and the first tulips,
more than petals,

were birds
I could arrange

inside, facing
out a window on trees

full of would-be
wings in wind

wanting to be birds.

I wanted a body
for the many feathers,

and for you to hold
the imagined-bird too.

I came as close
as I could

on the back road's
tarmac, flitting

from branch
to bare branch

shadow, out to the ends
of every limb,

wanting all I had,
my own shadow

cast behind me,
my wind-born

crown of hair, a nest
awaiting birds.

The Unexpected Aviary

All I was certain of at the beginning
was there was one about eiders.
Only now I find the preponderance of birds
presuming their places on every other
page. And the frames of windows.
And I want to say these discoveries
are good for something, evidence
there are within us unrealized images
binding our selves, performing
the work of quiet ringmasters.
Then I remembered the birds I forgot—
the hummingbird suspended at my ear,
the wind-wracked pelican, the stone
kingfisher. That nightingale finally
singing its heart outside my window
in 1987. It was dark as a crow's feather
in that room where I thought I was dreaming,
where I woke most nights in the snare
of those vultures, the nightmares.
There even the most dignified birds
were on their way to some terrible death,
while earthbound I railed and tried
but could not save them. And if it wasn't
the heron or the hawk, it was a fox
outside a window. Or the elk
I escort through rush-hour traffic
in an epic dream to safety.
But it *wasn't* safe, was it? I knew
reaching the threshold of the woods,
it was only a park. But, oh, that stretch,
that short breathtaking run and scent
through what seemed spacious.
I can tell you it's only stale if it is
on the page. How geese descended
Christmas day on a field inside locked gates
encircling the mental hospital.

How before comprehending migration,
we guessed they hid through winter
in the silt of lake bottoms.
My friend says any working theory
is good enough for a running start.
Perhaps it *was* the parakeet, pigeons,
no, the penguins in the zoo of childhood.
I knew the birds outside those windows
were all we had pointing to angels.
And I was going to know it.

Outside the Door

A fine rain of ice arrives after snow
at our doors. The door sticks,
frozen at first, in its frame.
You can throw yourself against it
then tug, both hands at the knob—
it might open to a disappearing
driveway, to sheathed forsythia
over this morning's toppled
birdfeeder. I've studied the ways
the squirrels wield their weight
and knock them down, while nuthatches
leer from the eaves, restationed
above a pair of pacing blue jays.
They're waiting to take *their* turn,
meanwhile the car won't start
to take me. The battery's dead
and, back inside, life isn't so easy either.
Every line's busy calling up neighbors
to borrow their cables. Here, need
is that cable between us, a snowplow
fitted to the mouth of the driveway.
I lost an earring out there between
my half-buried car and the icy
doorjamb, before the plow scooped it up
in a wall made of last night's
many inches. I had seen it missing
in the patch of my tilted
rearview mirror. In what has already
been shoveled aside, just buried,
it's already beginning to tarnish.
You could lose a fallen shovel
and wait out winter watching
the just-filled swinging feeders—
thinking and not thinking
of what's lost outside each door,
near enough and irretrievable.

Wallpaper

Purple finches at the feeder are actually purple in dusk light
behind those flourishing vines of frost overtaking
the window. Everything at once—last week and this week,

it will be next week's snowdrifts layered over the garden
behind this house a neighbor says the last owner moved into
during a sad-spell after her divorce. She left. She didn't.

So many sheets of flowered wallpaper had to be stripped
to get to the walls, every pattern barely different from the one
being covered. As if something new were being risked,

but only one small risk at a time. Or some mistake made,
you swore you wouldn't make again, that's made again,
slightly embellished the next time, or muted—

roses climbing a fence, followed by roses climbing a trellis,
followed by roses in free fall. Patterns festooned and spinning
at the eyes, dizzy as the dresses of women in the nursing home

where I stayed only as late to work as I had to, and that
too now, both here and another life I'm reaching twenty years
back for. Every door there required to be left opened.

I could walk down that corridor pitching goodnights
like bridal bouquets, or, roses—*Goodnight Dolores,*
Goodnight Albert. Goodnight Thelma. Thelma,

propped up every morning tied drooling to her wheelchair,
who was the hardest to look in the eye for all the resemblances.
She could have been the floral pattern just beneath me.

There can't be too many candles burning in a room,
something elemental in here, like the tree for Christmas,
its scent of balsam infiltrating the house. That tree,

and the painting near the window on the finally discovered
bare bedroom wall—of a woman receding, or maybe
emerging from a storm of Prussian blue, foundering

in the rose wash of dusk closer to purple—beside
a finch's breast disappearing into night, where the light
of day is followed by the light of candles taking over.

Rendezvous

It might be where you seat yourself
at the edge of the long wooden table—

a restless woman who can't sleep
in a house that is not her own

climbs downstairs, sits by chance
in the right chair, the precise angle,

in the world-before-dawn
when all form's still contour.

Some portion is choice. She wants
her back to the cold hearth,

her eyes addressing the window
where stenciled against an emerging sky

a ship's bell is bolted from a beam
above the porch. Picture only

a sliver of cloudless horizon—
the sun appearing beneath

the mouth of this bell, a burning
clapper dangling there for seconds.

The sun, as if perfectly forged,
hoists itself up into that rim

then isn't seen again,
by anyone, for days . . .

This could be a story about perspective.
Or the tale of a secret whispered

into an ear. A child hidden, curled
to fit the attic crawlspace.

Sun seeking asylum.
Cast the sun as the noiseless

ascension of the soul,
the bell, our hereafter.

That sun rose, a monk's
shaven head into the cowl,

a hummingbird lost inside
the foxglove. Maybe

not love with its tolling and fanfare—
but each image, once given,

received and permitted to live
in imagination.

Sightings

1.

Crows skim over a page of snow
behind the house
as if one sentence were enough.

One sentence
can claim
everything counts.

Shingles tier on the barn
mimicking rows of wing feathers

stained the color of that Burgundy
he passed with a late night kiss
from his mouth filling mine.

2.

Have I already said their daily
arrivals

were compelling
as their inevitable disappearances?

Their day-to-day work
exposing us

to weightlessness?

Our bodies are the splintered stakes
we're tied to.

Everything counts.

Nailed over the bed
of my earliest childhood friend,

the cross was a sparrow
with stiff wings
the first time I saw it.

3.

It was late April and the storefront
door, wide open,

a starling trapped inside one room
full of handmade dollhouses
and miniatures.

It flew like that store was on fire,

from roof to roof, tiny kitchen to parlor,
toppling a cradle,

against a pane of glass—

the owner shrieking
as I walked in
at her only customer.

Remembering how,
I threw my green sweater
over it, carried that heartbeat

wrapped in my hands
across the threshold

where it did what I counted on,
flew off into a sycamore without us.

4.

At Long Lake the heron was camouflaged
right there before our eyes.

Then, smack of wings, shot out,
our canoe barely rocking
that acre

of pickerelweed
and waterlilies.

We fly without wings in our dreams,

break into morning
through the bulrushes of sleep
where we find what we'll count on.

5.

I woke to a beady-eyed titmouse
drumming at a seed between its feet,

to one day unfettered
by the small or greater sorrows
always here to choose from.

I woke to the nose-dive
dips of chickadees,

to a choir of birds,
unaccountably happy.

6.

Have I counted on them
for companionship? Yes.

And when there weren't birds
I turned to wind.

Wind, too, can turn air

from vacant space
into some live element.

7.

Remember how gestureless
we felt on the banks of the Delaware?
No fluttering anywhere.

It was a day we couldn't account for,
the air and river breathless—

even the ducks became stones on stones,
so motionless we nearly believed in it.

8.

Our world's total avian population
was last reckoned at about 100 billion—
give or take some hundreds of millions.

Do you wonder what makes us count?

How many have passed overhead
casting their passing shadows over you?

9.

At the crest of the hill
before the orchard,

a weathervane bent
by countless storms

back almost off its perch—

copper rooster and arrow
aimed now
accidentally skyward.

10.

How I woke with the word
ceaseless in my mouth.

Ceaseless, ceaseless,
ceaseless—

like a bird dealt one phrase
among all others for a lifetime.
Then, counting on it.

II

The Crossing

It is not always like this—
November stampeding through leafless limbs,
my ears shut up inside
where it is never warm enough.
I have not heard my voice
in my own voice for this whole season,
only strangers scrambling out
to cross the road—
like small dead animals
we see and then try not to see.
I once said all the wrong things
but knew them as mine. Now,
there is only this stuttering over apologies
and the mouthing of hymns
one line behind the others.
You cannot speak for me,
but when you speak I believe
it is you that is speaking.
This sees me across.

Hand to Mouth

Like the hand of Job cupped to his mouth—

our irrepressible gesture
in the face of dark news, improbable beauty,
anything larger than we might have imagined
one moment earlier—

mate to gasping.

During Bach's *Toccata and Fugue*, birds
swoop as shadows behind the stained church window,
sifting down through Mary's crown
nestling into her lap—

the apostles' eyes, fixed Godward
for all these years, satisfied—

my hand rising, as if called, to my mouth.

Like drawing the conch to an ear, some message
concerning awe transmitted between them.
Involuntary as breath, or tears—

speaking for the unspeakable.

Bird Calls

1.

Who wouldn't root for it, clutched
against common sense above traffic,
small finch to an aspen's slimmest branch—
wind whipped up, zipper of lightning,
thunder? We're fixed on its body
through the cafe's second-floor window,
fingers tightening like tendrils
through our cup handles. Looking up
from the page, we're all losing our places.

2.

In that morning stupor, the chair
by the window, the window
to the street where the shadow of a bird,
I'd guess pigeon, swayed so long
on a wire I lurched when the green
Chevy rattling past the house
ran it over. I loved that woman who flew
out the fourteenth story, the only note
she left, a darkening stain
on cement beneath a window.

3.

The chicks are in the pan, mama's cooking
them alive. No one in the dream
kitchen can stop her or leave the table.
We don't look them or each other
in the eye. We stare out at a neighbor
staring out at us from a window.

4.

The train chugs north. Outside
the measure of a green tinted window,
a heron wades camouflaged
within bulrushes, marsh lilies, trash.
You want to blame somebody.
Reckless Bird Hits Windshield.
Once, I was driving. Once
I was speeding away, spitting
bitter accusations at a small black bird,
at my dozing passengers.

5.

What surprises us most is that we have
something they want, something
in cupped palms upturned
for alms beside the pasture. Bluebirds,
swallows circling. Meadowlarks
taking turns perched on our wrists.
This surprises us more in the dream
than knowing God is watching from a window.

6.

We keep eyeing the window for the promised
snow. Count thirty evening grosbeaks
settled like tropical fruit in one maple's
generous bare branches.
We did nothing to deserve this. The sky
holds back its downfall. There must be
someone throttling the tree—ripened birds
then, all at once, their capricious uprising.

Dreaming of the Front Lines

The mattress is laid outdoors
as if this were natural.

I am speaking to a friend
on a phone, my legs still tangled
in the knot of a cool cotton sheet.

I describe to her in detail
the sumptuousness of the hibiscus
flowering above the mattress,
a tree heavy with red leafy blossoms
like drowsy birds perched
all together in a breeze.

Some swoop soundlessly down.

My first lover sleeps beside me,
the one so deliberately kind.

Then the invasion begins,
hundreds of soldiers in khaki uniforms
dropping like blossoms,
parachuting from the sky—

as many soldiers as blossoms
landing feet first, heads
snapping left, snapping right.

They trudge in heavy boots
off after each other, trampling
the fallen hibiscus,

marching toward the front lines
which are always nearby.

January 15th

It wasn't you. It wasn't,
until I entered the date
at the top of the page,
what I always do
to fasten myself first
to the world with the pen.
It wasn't until I said
the lip-seamed *M* at the start
heading to the inevitable
double *L's* at the end,
Michelle, the word shell
for the first time sounding
itself inside there.
It wasn't the shell dropping
when I pictured it
again, something someone
might have caught
looking out a window
at nightfall turning
in the center of January.
It wasn't your long
unbroken fall
from the fourteenth story
yanking thirty years later
at the rip cord
of my life. It wasn't you
pitched by what
we call *choice*
out a window, the only
close call being
how it hadn't been me.
It wasn't you leaving
me shattered and determined
never to shatter, and it was.

Nightmares

Common as flies on a roadkill—

all day swerving from
weariness, from everything standing

for everything else.
Dying of thirst, the heron

won't drink from the saucer.
The hawk survives but with only one wing.

My sister who can't believe
I can't remember

says, squirreling into the arm of the couch,
Every day . . . what do you want me to say?

Every day bared in nightmares.
No help. No help. All help a dress

laced with straight pins at the hem
yanked over the head.

Take it off, mama said,
(pressing a thread between my lips

keeps her from sewing up my brains)
and later, *How was I supposed to know?*

What was it I could not tell her?

Two foxes are trapped in a sack
on the road, one's still breathing.

The zipper is jammed. The car
heading toward us is speeding.

The sky is falling out of the sky
in hunks, like pond ice calving.

The Daily Work of Forgetting

If she did not exist, she wouldn't notice.

If she crouched beneath the forsythia bushes
in the small front lawn.

If she rode her bicycle faster than the stray dog,
she wouldn't notice. If she could sleep.

If she could know God, she thought, she wouldn't
notice. She would have Him to talk to.

She'd talk. She'd make up what He would say.

He'd say, *Stay with me now and I will make
things right for you later.*

If she made her bed. If she found a boy
and eked a drug out of their lust.

If she fed her crusts to birds.

If she forgot each day as soon as it was over.

The Great Loneliness

It would begin in the chest

as a dull pressure
accompanying prayers—

a chilled draft
persisting
at the back of the neck.

Each day would be pursued
by the nagging conviction

we had forgotten something.

In sleep, we'd dream of the antelope
and the whale and not know

who they were, waking
as from a reunion with our dead

to their vanishing faces.

Bourbon would be useless
for comfort. Sex, our allotted

outpost of wilderness,
interrupted by glimpses

of an indescribable
breadth of absence.

That one swallow
sweeping the summer sky,

appearing like a crust of bread
after weeks of only water.

Burying the Dog

The way Gandhi or any saint
might be attended to the last,

that's how she died. My offering
the shallow white saucer to her mouth,

her lapping then sleeping
then panting through the night.

She was the one who never
used words. Blue-red tongue

thin as flame across my wrist—
she'd lick and lick as if

to say, *Listen, it's beating.*

When they said it was no use
digging at frozen ground in February,

I borrowed the neighbor's pickaxe
and learned how to throw a wide swing

to the grave. I knew love
had forced more than the earth

to open in winter. And flint
after flint after flint

that ground flew back at me
like all griefs.

March 30th

The body knows how to breathe—

this morning when I woke
mine was ushering the air
of the bedroom,

with only
its two small windows,
through me.

And what
was I asked for
in return?

Each window bears
its vision of the world. Here
snow still falls,

ushered for hours
by the sky
through the body of the sky

that knows how,
that *how*

we must be hardwired to ask
as we are to breathe
and to gasp

at so much light
bestowed on our tired,
noble branches.

All is asked
in return.

I will have to go out into it
breathing, because

the feeders are empty,
my body knows how.

And each goldfinch,
who asks nothing
but returns, is molting

feather by gray feather,

growing gradually
into its true name,

every body within
its body
knowing how.

Mute Swans

That's when I began collecting feathers—

crossing over the stone bridge of the Public Gardens
where they were camped on banks around the pond

preening, each the center of a shadow
white as parachutes they hadn't yet stepped out of.

I had no intentions, but my hands did—
plucking feathers from grass, hoarding feathers

in my bag, and I let them. Hands-turned-beggars,
approaching one Mute swan, then the next.

There was another woman foraging
in a trash barrel nearby, so I heard her

ask me what it was I planned to do with them.
This was no place for answers. Then later,

had one, *I don't know*. But why was I whispering?

I wasn't hurting anything, and they were busy,
permitting me closer than you'd think.

I must have been wearing my huge black carry-all
because it was before my shoulder gave out

lugging all those books I might need a sentence
or page from at a moment's notice.

Maybe one or two feathers worth.

This was during one of the wars of our lifetime
when reports of scorched soldiers and birds

arrived in the same breath on the morning radio,
and I'd collapse, folding my head beneath

the too-easy wings of *I can't bear it.* That's when
I molted for, maybe, good. I saw it—

the *I won't* in the *I can't,* and dropped a whole suit
of plumage edging on to the question, *how can I?*

It was the end of a week and we were all disheveled.

Twenty-five thousand feathers to each,
and even they were momentarily flightless.

A bird's feathers can weigh more than their bones.

There were more feathers than there was light
when I made my way home.

III

The Act of Sweeping

A woman is sweeping her porch
as if life depended on it,

dowsing for counsel
through the press

of an old broom, through
some small sure act

she can be certain
does no harm.

Wind rouses, loosening leaves
from even the stiffest branches,

and sets the tiny
green boat on the bay

rocking like our wavering
scales of justice.

She could be paddling
herself across. Wind

sweeps the porch. A crow
who walked the plank

bobs on one quivering
wrist of pine—

springs off, as if to dive,
but rises.

Back Road to the Orchard

I am that woman they reported
feeling sorry for, waking
alone to the house-of-every-morning
making so much of the company
of birds, carrying
breakfast back to bed
beside the carved Tibetan figure
whose hands meet perpetually
in prayer, its soles
taped to the nightstand
to keep it from falling
on its face again.
I am the woman with no children
leading neighborhood children
in the promised, annual
carrot-pulling brigade
where on our knees inside the garden
we all look up and claim
to see it—one dispersing,
threadbare angel
sketched against sky
out of vapor and wind.
I am the woman rebuilding
the four steps to the porch,
where rips in the screen
are patched with squares
of screen—the one traipsing
past dusk up this hill,
interrupting, like any animal,
the beam of your headlights.
I am that woman,
setting out for it day after day,
reaching the orchard
and catching my breath
before swerving home again.

The Carpenter's Son

When the carpenter's six-year-old son Uriah
picks out a music box from a carton in my attic,

I tell him it's broken.

He opens the lid, winding the already overworked key,
and the minuet I haven't heard for twenty years
plucks its tin-pan song.

I'm a Christian, he says, as if by way of explanation.

The word broken means nothing to him.

God's in your music box, he announces, as we climb
down complaining stairs, and he trails me out
cupping it like a nestling he sets down inside the garden.

He watches me untangle, then carefully stake
each heavy, pungent vine.

God's in your tomato plants, he says.
Still, I break some.

Then he draws through his believing fingers
the tail of every blue-grained ribbon I spliced and knotted
around the fence for discouraging birds.

The word discourage means nothing to birds.

You know, he says, *God's in your ribbons.*

Blue Mountain, Autumn

We can't eavesdrop on every creation
at once.

Conversations multiply in this wind.

Each crest of the lake, a thin upper lip
where light is carried.

Each trough, a shadow, a mouth
slightly opened.

Several words break
here on the dock pilings—

> *leave anguish behind . . .*
>
> *every parting*
> *braved*
>
> *is a flat-sided stone*
> *for the footbridge*
> *over the brook . . .*
>
> *every grief unwept,*
> *a coyote*
> *lodged in the throat . . .*

When the notebook is left open on the dock,
wind turns the pages.

Window of Sixteen Panes

The red fox recrossed the field—
as if tracing a five-pointed star,
lost in grief, black-pawed,
or pursuing the trickster voice
of its prey that ricocheted, *Here*,
and then, *No, over here, behind you.*

Whatever raised my eyes
from the book, from the world
of the word that just said,
all splits open . . .
we witness . . . to see this fox
padding back and forth

through all the panes
of the window? Stepping
freely out of one pane
it slips into the measured
frame of another, annulling
the authority of these borders

staked between territories—
between this afternoon
and the fenced yard of childhood,
loose weave of chainlink
charting plots of sky. From life,
into the country after.

      *   *   *

Striding up the dirt road
that worked separate fields
out of one field, split them in two—
the hem of a painter's
long blue coat flaps
from her ankles in wind, or maybe

not wind, only the wavering
in that pane of old warped glass
she is now passing through—
like a woman calf-high in a river,
plowing a furrow of air.
The slope of the horizon

is a curvature, interrupted.
The spruce occupies seven panes.
A chicory sky bleeds into five.
The painter and chameleon clouds
commute like the red fox
between them.

                  ★   ★   ★

Light careens, she says,
into her studio without knocking,
spills onto one painting
as collaborator. A body of light
flung in perfect proportions
to curl itself into the lap

of an empty armchair only
outlined on the fresh canvas. As if
absence drew presence, rose
and aureolin shimmering there, uninvited
but welcome, and then disappeared
crossing back into the woods.

                  ★   ★   ★

Slim branches of bare birch
break each of the highest panes
down against the sky.
Dragonfly sight. Casings
splitting up the all
into manageable-size portions.

Resting my eyes on the bare wall,
there's a honeycomb of sixteen
dark square chambers.
An afterimage: what is not, is.
Sixteen thresholds. And if the door
of the room opens, seventeen.

*　　　*　　　*

The black piping of stained
church windows, affixing glass
for the pleasure of squandering color.
The trees lay their shadows
down across the road—dark fronds
that totter in wind, like each

new day now of March, a gate
swinging on its hinges back and forth
between seasons. The red fox
trails a chain of tracks in snow
over the boot prints of a woman.
The crow swoops through nine panes.

*　　　*　　　*

Entrusting her way in the dark
to the road, that road between fields
the painter has faith leads home
beneath her. Hearing a snap,
the faint shuffle, she turns.
The moon's new. The red fox

is out hunting. Behind her,
the window of sixteen panes—
a calendar of light burning
measures of time. The red fox sees
what must be the chamber
where day is held confined

until morning: a silhouette
corralled into six panes
turns off the light. The red fox
and the painter and I and the fields
sprawl in the dark beyond
the cloister of the body—

beneath that boundless rim
we've named sky to contain us.

Intermediaries

It came over me in the orchard—

acres of apple trees blossoming
and I have walked into the thick of them.

There, I only know they are beautiful
the way you know anything
from a great distance.

On the outskirts of the orchard is one young poplar

doing what poplars do
in a rising and falling wind,
quivering and being still again.

It takes the poplar to deliver me
into the lusciousness of the orchard.

Once, in one of the famous churches
of Florence, I followed a path
into a small hidden courtyard

and startled an old woman
in a kerchief watering geraniums.

I had only heard of the spirit
in that church, the way I'd first
known the beauty of the orchard.

Looking at the poplar, I remembered this woman

asking me to fill her pail with water
and pass it back to her, and how, later,
I entered the church upon reentering it.

Birds were appearing and disappearing
into and out of the orchard's blossoms.

I wanted to tell you this.

The poplar and the woman
standing on a chair in her kerchief
to reach the geraniums—they did

what the birds have always
managed for me.

Driving Into Rapture

Just south of Castleton Corners
the highway bends and they take over,
mountains circling like gods
conferring on you your real size—
one small coin in the offering plate
lined with green felt. Somehow spared,
farmland sprawls the foothills.

And maybe that's where it begins,
with a man's bare back, hunkered over,
sweating in sun under a sparrow-studded sky.
He's plucking wild blueberries, or
laying the old cranky barncat to rest.
You know him. He's digging up
some treasure he buried as a child
for safekeeping. He wants to hold it now.

Or, maybe it's the figurehead of clouds,
the accompaniment on the radio,
yours now, the dark body of the cello,
and wind threading the windows,
when suddenly you're flooded
with all the sweetest moments of your life,
no matter how they turned or soured later.

That's when it stops short in front of you,
Ford Pickup, muffler shot,
six scruffy kids scrapping out back—
when there isn't one jaded hair left
on your disbelieving head, its rusty bumper
plastered with stickers all certain,
God Loves You, Don't Worry God Loves You.

Testimony

So, it happens. Longing no longer
presiding over everything.
Fill the feeder, birds come.

Mourning doves emancipated
from their names: ringing each eye,

the almost missed rim
of baby blue.

*

Babies. There would have been two.
See them fussing to make
a nest out of my lap,

that empty begging bowl. Brimming,
those failures no longer
astonish me. Even that pasture, the bed

with only night after night after . . .
How little has become enough.

I light what's left,
the stub of a white candle.

*

Bonfire. The New Year's invitation
reads, *Bring what you want
to leave behind. Watch it burn.*

*

Recognize that heat? Driving
north, the frame of a car
on the highway swallowed

at midnight in flames.
The question of did they get out
in time? *I was that. I did that.*

I did. Sung as facts—
the peal of self-reproachments
retired to another country.

*

Without any flag, the pole
in front of a motel just past Derry—
stark spire cut out of the dark

by floodlights. A tapering wand
held perfectly still
in the raised hand of the conductor

between movements.
All that suspense.

Says it's possible, this round
of reckoning—the hauled
out, the standing up,

the staggering forth,
amazed. Mid-life
the itinerary

changes. Good thing.
The next exit is ours.

IV

Notes from Eagle Island

1.

The trouble was the trouble
always faced in paradise—

so much *other*
and,

how to enter?

2.

The mailboat captain rows us
from his anchored ferry
to a cusp of sand at shore

where you and I
and our ballast of cartons
are hoisted overboard.

He shouts at us,
into wind, pushing out

before I hear
his warning.

So, already it's us
pitted against
the incoming tide—

rushed lugging what we belong to
off the beach to the door
of the farmhouse

up through sea cliffs, hedges
of sea rose, purple thistle,
grass waist-high.

3.

Imagine, instructions.

There's a sheaf on the kitchen table.

Uncovering the well, where the kerosene's shelved,
a penciled sketch of countless paths.

How rain rattles off the roof
down to fill the cellar cistern.

What not to bury, what to bury.
What to burn.

What not to burn.

Didn't it all appear more
frivolous from the mainland?

Every window but one here's
hawking its version
of field-ridge-sea-shoals-sky.

We have come to unmoor ourselves
from ourselves—

spend days stuttering,
Beautiful, Beautiful,

as if each rationed that one word.

4.

Cornered in this vastness,
you can unpack.

But pressed between books,
wrapped in the folds
of towels, sleeves and socks,

are stowaways:
your every-grief-worth-brooding-over.

5.

I'm forging fellowship wherever I can,
with the broken wooden door—

its torn screen flaps, upper sash barely hinged,
knocked clattering with every passage.

On the sill of a window—
that midnight-blue creamer
hand-painted with orange dahlias
around the rim

where a hairline crack begins
running down
through to the bottom—

it can't hold on to anything for long.

There is too much to hold, but as if there isn't
enough, we waste no time, revert

on our very first walk to longing—
croon to see the island through falling snow,

plotting over obstacles
to our next possible
trip back here.

The book says awe is always some blend
of beauty and terror, making sensible

how we recruited God
as chaperone—

because before you invent eyes,
pasting faces on every thing here,
to look back at you,

it's all sheets draped over shining mirrors.

6.

Our eyes are nomads,
but pacing this beach

mine are fixed on the few inches
surrounding each step,

homing in on something
I'll only know
when I see it—

as those left homeless
after a hurricane
hunt for recognizable scraps
in the rubble, some thing

to vouch
for who they are.

From that schooner in the distance,
I could be a knickknack
orphaned on a shelf of sand—

a stiff-jointed doll that blinks.

You could only use the word *peaceful*
if you weren't looking.

Simply standing still here at the edge,
your bare feet can be taken
from beneath you,

burrowed with each departing wave
deeper and deeper.

7.

All afternoon, the festering argument
between the sea and the shore,
surf clobbering the cliffs.

How gradually you can begin to believe
you belong here.

The tide turns its back
on a bed of glistening stones: islands
whittled to miniatures.

Concessions are strewn every day
along a newly drawn margin.

8.

Hiking all day the periphery of the island,
I can't help but fall into seeing
for both of us,

threading every brush with the sublime
into a rosary of details
to carry back to you—

assembling companionship
like this on the spot,

the way we stake vines
or heavy-headed blossoms
in the garden

to keep them from snapping
at the stem

under the weight of what alone
is unbearable.

This is why Adam and undoubtedly
Eve began to name things.
Not to conquer—

but to bear what paradise suggested to each
in the other's absence.

So they could tell each other.

9.

Monks hood. Sumac.
Inkberry.

I am working to see
only one thing at a time—

the preponderance
of that single image
throughout the woods,

one tall pine
fallen into the arms
of another.

10.

Seams open in the sky
and the sun puts down rays around us
like tent poles.

I say, *there must be a name for this.*

You say, *Godlight.*

The clouds are blues unfurling blues
on paler blues—and

this is how it might look,
the deepening of a trail of thought.

Blues unfurling blues
on paler blues

translucent as the powder
of moths' wings.

11.

From a dirt road cutting
through a field
at the heart of the island,
I think I've discovered
one renegade Chinese poppy
full-open in a wash
of summer grasses.
Then, its petals
disperse—tearing up and off
into a hundred
specks of tangerine.
The monarchs are migrating,
convening here to feed
on the whitened pedestals
of blossoming valerian.
Our eyes are known for this,
for making mistakes.

12.

The only reason for my ungainly plunge
was—

you made it look possible,
your body shouting up for me

to imagine past the cold
of the cove
to weightlessness.

13.

Moon as scimitar.

The hour of last light.

I scavenge for the revelation
lurking in every form.

The darkening woods
calls you to declare
what you believe in—

I took the wrong trail
at the crossroad.

My body is torn
between the fear of being
lost, and the work
of finding my way home—

between the impulse to run
and the impulse to kneel.

14.

A ship with coal-gray sails
inches into view across that tightrope
the horizon.

You say, *let it stand*
for the grace of darkness.

I say, *the sky is falling.*

As rips in the ozone widen,

what will become of what we know
as light? As color?

It's the somber woman
in that fresco
dressed in black,

critics have argued over
for centuries. Who is she?

I say, *she knows what's coming.*

You say, *that ship's become*
the vanishing point.

15.

We find what is most urgent
to find in the dream

where you are on your knees
on the beach somewhere behind me

holding up wedges of tumbled sea-glass
as if they were the chipped
points of stars,

worshiping only the light
that passes through them

as I work my way out
to the head of the bluff carrying
nothing but that question—

*Who says we're entitled
to refuge?*

Surf smacks the stone face
shattering a clear bottle
into a flume of many-colored pieces.

And, *Every loss is not betrayal.*

That's when I let go of the invisible
guard-rail, the one I've been
gripped to all my life,

edging back with both hands
free to tell you.

16.

We are children of these accidental, but
nevertheless, communions.

The loon wakes me. Sound of one voice
and another that answers,
tremolo saturating the August air
for miles.

I haul myself up, wooden bucket full
from the well.

On neighboring islands, others
are drawing themselves
half-willingly from sleep

to hear the wailing of two birds, a calling
we have no choice but to share in the night,

blackened as the glass chimney
on the kerosene lamp, the wick
gone too long untrimmed.

17.

Our friend's child once said,
We are all underwater
and the angels are fishing for us.

And what are they using for bait?

He claims, *Birds.*

18.

In that small cradle of a boat
we wait scanning the surface in silence,

as if keeping some appointment we once made.

We are hungry for something larger
than the sighting of seals
inside the sighting of seals.

That first head emerges—crowning
dark clump of clay

still dripping wet
from the hands of the maker.

Then, the language of eyes locked to eyes.
Our first language.

And all of us, fingerprints.

19.

All week, that unsettling odor we can't locate,
but something's rotten in paradise.

Where the pans are stored
we find what's left of a dead vole
under the lid of a lobster pot

and look at each other
ungenerously.

That's why the body doesn't just get tossed,
together we feel obliged
to make the time for ceremony.

We bury it in the woods behind the house
on top of a mound, the way Bedouins
interred their dead, to be closer to heaven.

20.

Sprawled at dawn in the Adirondack chair
beside the house, I'm waiting for the sun to lift up
at the opposite side of this island,

casting a strip of first light on a shoal out in the bay
before making the ever-slow crossing toward us—

sweeping tide, with no intention of stopping
at the tideline—up the beach, ledges,
reaching my bare outstretched feet.

When my ankles are taken, so are the stones
we arranged yesterday in a ring on the grass.

A crow paddles air overhead as light's
cupped to kneecaps.

When the heat settles above my thighs in the pool
of my lap, it makes a mirror out of the window
to the room where you are still sleeping.

Light splashed, a fine shawl drawn
across bare shoulders, then covering the wings
of an open notebook on the weathered table.

I once knew someone who would say,
So, what's the point? So what?

So, I'm always braced for this question.

The point is, grace is indiscriminate. Or,
sensual pleasure has its own brand of intelligence.

The point is, anticipation. Or, light shed
gratuitously on the wing, the body, the chair.

When my hips were taken, two cormorants flew
in tandem with each other and their shadows.

The point is, I made nothing more of it.

Or, how everything can be moving unself-consciously
through light, while you sit outside that rim
in the chilled observing shadow.

The point is, bees dive into the opened mouths
of roses, noisy as infants to the nipple,

and the moon's a bleached sand dollar
still swaddled in ample blue.

Contingencies.

The point is, light gathers up the dispossessed
and soon I'll have to move or this heat
will be too much for me.

Or, well, what is it *you* worship?

The point is a stony ledge
with an ever-changing face.

21.

Once a day the herring gull rises in a chute of air
above these ledges and drops its sea urchin
over and over again.

Every day, to get to the meat,
it shatters *Aristotle's lantern.*

22.

No one would believe how we went on
praying for that fog, that emblem of soured vacations
on the summer coast of Maine.

We needed a reprieve from our
record-breaking stretch of perfect weather,

the daily demands that we relate or not
to every surface, its reflection
and its shadow.

It wasn't only the chill it would bring,
justifying a fire in the wood stove.

I knew we shouldn't want this,
but we did—

all foreground, a world
where everything out of reach

had to be taken on faith
still existed.

Raking clams on the mud flat of low tide,
I turn as if hearing the bank of fog approach.

It rolls in thick across the Penobscot
baptizing blindly,

even more evenhandedly than light.

23.

Slackwater. The sea performing its impersonation
of quiet. Unriffled acres turning the color
of mulled red wine.

All day the light hangs as if evenly dissolved
in a solution of air, then falls at dusk
from the sky out of its mysterious suspension.

We watch the sun shrink toward the horizon,
rayed nimbus hovering just above the head of a saint.

It floats for an indisputably long time in a nest
of spruce on the facing island, opaque
and tiny as a porch light, then appears to disappear.

We turn away toward what one of us absentmindedly
calls *home*. We say, *It's all over.*

But the sun rises again for seconds, thrown up
for an encore, hesitant as anyone who has trouble
saying goodbyes.

24.

The book says, *The self is no mystery,*
the mystery is that there is
something for us to stand on.

The stone embedded
in the dirt path
shifts beneath my foot.

From the bluff at the end of this road,
the mainland's a decoy
in the distance we'd fallen for.

25.

Wanting to surprise you the way the sun did,
throw doubt on what we call *endings,*

I left you packing alone in the house
knowing you'd forgive me later

and snuck out down the path to the lighthouse
where I found what I was looking for,
and also the unexpected—those raspberries

we thought wouldn't ripen until we'd left,
fat and dropping almost uncoaxed.

I stuffed my mouth with that sweet-tart fruit,
and my jacket pockets with what I'd come for—

handfuls of sea-rose petals
that gave themselves up as easily.

On the way back, I met the snake in the road
slithering through its own unmoving curves
off into the brush.

This is why I was late and you were already
loading the boat when I got there, too busy
sighing about leaving to mention it.

26.

Half-way out that bay to the mainland, I was too busy
too, brimming with that uncomplicated affection

it's only possible to feel saying goodbye to a place.
Busy forgetting, until I caught my hands

stained from fruit the color of roses
and pulled them out, squandering roses into wind

toward the island dwindling behind us.
So I surprised myself too—

petals swirling and landing on the surface water,
swooping at the boat like gulls trailing fish trawls,

petals blown with spray back up at us,
planting badges on our sleeves and pasting

kisses to that look of disbelief on your face
that says both, *How do we come by such pain?*

How do we come by such pleasure?
It was a kind of toast wasn't it—

grace spoken at the end of one meal
and the beginning of what we hope

might be another? We're like the shipwrecked
in that story, who wait and wait for a message

that doesn't come, then comes, from a great
blue heron who could mean anything

calling down to them—*Hold fast. Hold fast.*
There's more.

Dedication page: The epigraph is taken from Rainer Maria Rilke's, *Duino Elegies* (translated by Stephen Mitchell).

Page 13: The title of this poem was inspired by Toni Morrison's, *Nobel Lecture in Literature* (1993).

Page 20: The conspiracy of the table, bell and window were gifts of the Blue Mountain Center. The poem is dedicated to Karen Latuchie.

Page 29: This poem is dedicated to Jane Cooper.

Page 34: This poem is dedicated to the life and memory of Michelle Marie Mazeppa.

Page 35: My grandmother Lillian brought a trove of superstitions with her from Russia that were passed along to her children and grandchildren. One of these concerned the necessity of holding a thread in one's mouth if you were wearing a piece of clothing while it was being mended, "so as not to sew up your brains."

Page 38: The poem was inspired by a statement attributed to Chief Seattle, 1854, "If all the beasts were gone man would die from a great loneliness."

Page 47: I am grateful to Alice Nye who inspired this poem, and to whom it is dedicated.

Page 51: "All splits open . . . we witness," is taken from Muriel Rukeyser's poem, *After The Quarrel*, from her book, *Body of Waking*. I am grateful to Catherine Drabkin, who appears in this poem, for the inspiration of her story and her painting, *One Chair*.

Page 62: These poems are dedicated to Patricia Wilczynski whose companionship helped inspire them. I remain grateful, also, to Virginia and Tom Slayton who first invited me to Eagle Island.

Page 77: The "woman in black" appears in Giotto's fresco, *Meeting at the Golden Gate*, in the Arena Chapel in Padua.

Page 80: I am grateful to Adam Filleul-Crawford for his insight and imagination.

Page 85: "Aristotle's lantern" is a small structure within the shell of the sea urchin that was first described as resembling a lantern by Aristotle in his, *Historia Animalium*.

Page 88: "The self is no mystery . . ." is taken from George Oppen's poem, *World, World*, from his *Collected Poems*.

Acknowledgments are also due to the editors of the following publications in whose pages some of the poems in this book first appeared.

The American Literary Review Driving Into Rapture

The American Voice Back Road to the Orchard

The Beloit Poetry Journal Sightings, Notes from Eagle Island

Blueline Blue Mountain, Autumn

Convergence The Carpenter's Son

Descant Dreaming of the Front Lines, Hand to Mouth, Nightmares,
    That Great Loneliness, Window of Sixteen Panes

Flint Hills Review The Crossing, Wallpaper, Intermediaries

The Granite Review The Act of Sweeping

Gulf Coast The Unexpected Aviary, January 15th, Bird Calls

Ladies Start Your Engines: Women Writers on Cars & The Road (Faber & Faber 1997)
    Driving Into Rapture

Poets On Burying the Dog

Prairie Schooner The Birds That Are Not in Our Hands,
    The Daily Work of Forgetting

Turning Wheel The Act of Sweeping

Under the Legislature of Stars (Oyster River Press)
    The Carpenter's Son